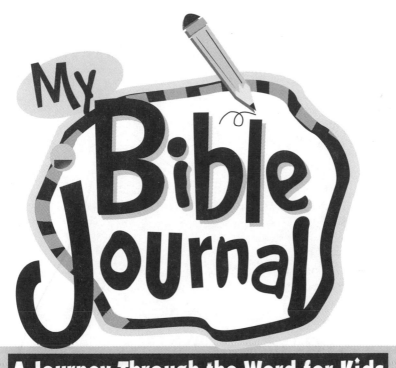

A Journey Through the Word for Kids

Mary J. Davis

An imprint of Hendrickson Publishers Marketing, LLC.
Peabody, Massachusetts
www.HendricksonRose.com

To Larry
To Jeff, Pam and Shelbee
To Wendi and Jack
I love all you guys!

My Bible Journal
©2014 by Mary J. Davis

RoseKidz®
An imprint of Hendrickson Publishers Marketing, LLC.
P. O. Box 3473, Peabody
Massachusetts 01961-3473
www.HendricksonRose.com

Register your book at www. HendricksonRose.com/register and receive a free Bible Reference download.

Interior Illustrator: Aline Heiser

ISBN 10: 1-885358-70-9
ISBN 13: 978-1-885358-70-7
RoseKidz® reorder#: L46911
Juvenile Nonfiction / Religion / Devotion & Prayer

Printed in the United States of America   [16] 05.2017.VP

Table of Contents

Introduction

I have hidden your word in my heart that I might not sin against you.
— Psalm 119:11

Did you know that the Bible is written for kids like you? Whether you like adventure stories, romances, mysteries or comedy, you can find it in the Bible. And while you're at it, you will learn about important ways to live. As you work through each activity you will find out more and more about the Bible. Plus you will grow closer to God!

Get to know God's heroes, and the unlikely characters God used to instruct and guide His people. Write down your thoughts and dreams. Journey through the Bible. Before you know it, you will have read the whole Bible — God's special gift to you.

My Bible Journal is written to help you learn what is in God's Word. You will read from each book of the Bible. To make the best use of *My Bible Journal*, follow these steps:

Where Are We?

This is the "address" part of the lesson. You will be asked to read some of these chapters later in "Digging In," or you can stop at this section and read all of the chapters or the book listed.

What's the Big Picture?

This will give you an idea of what the book or partial book is about. Keep this information in mind while working on this section.

Who Are the Main Players?

Many people are presented in most of the books of the Bible. A list of the main characters in the lesson will help you learn to recognize Bible people.

Digging In

This is where you will read parts of the Bible. One or more main stories will be listed for you to read. Read all of the suggested verses. Think about what the story or event means to you. Write your answers, ideas and thoughts on the lines provided.

Digging Deeper

This section gives you even more of God's Word to explore. You may complete this section now, or you could stop here and come back another day to learn more about this particular book of the Bible.

Plant God's Word

This is your memory verse. Write it down and put it where you can see it each day. Repeat it often.

Glossary

A special dictionary of terms for *My Bible Journal* begins on page 147. If you see a word in the reading that you do not understand, look in the Glossary. If it is not there, look in a Bible dictionary or a regular dictionary.

That's it! All of the lessons follow these steps, except for the first one. It is an overview of the Bible that shows you how the Bible is set up. After that, every lesson uses the sections above.

Won't it be easy to read through the Bible? Get started now!

If anyone obeys his word, God's love is truly made complete in him. This is how we know we are in him.

— 1 John 2:5

Old Testament

What Is the Bible?

Look at the table of contents for your Bible. The Bible has 66 books.

There are two divisions in the Bible. They are called the _____ Testament and the _____ Testament.

The Old Testament has _____ books.

The New Testament has ____ books.

Who wrote the Bible? Look up 2 Timothy 3:16 to find the answer: Several people held a pen and wrote the words, but _____ inspired every word in the Bible.

The Old Testament

There are four divisions in the Old Testament. These divisions are called: _____

_____

Law

The first five books tell about God the creator, His dealings with people, and the laws He gave to guide people. Write the names of the five books of law here. _____

_____

History

The next 12 books tell the history of God's people, and point to a redeemer who will come. Write the names of the 12 books of history here. _____

_____

Poetry

These five books begin with Job. You will learn of others' experiences as God reveals Himself to the world. You will read psalms and praises to God. You will learn some wise ways to live and some ways to please God. Write the names of the five books of poetry here. (Remember that these five books begin with Job.) _____

⭐ _____

Prophecy

There are 17 books of prophecy. You will learn what God says concerning His people and His Son, Jesus. The books of prophecy tell how God's own people failed to remain faithful to Him many times. However, God still loved His people enough to send His Son to redeem us all. Write the names of the 17 books of prophecy here. _____

_____

_____

The New Testament

There are four divisions in the New Testament. The divisions are called: _____

_____

Gospels

These four books tell all about Jesus, from His birth to His ascension into heaven. Write the names of the four Gospels here._____

_____

History

There is only one book of history in the New Testament. It tells about the beginning of the church. It is called _____ .

Letters

Also called epistles, these 21 books teach how to live as Christians. They give strength, faith and hope. Write the names of the 21 letters._____

_____

_____

Prophecy

There is only one New Testament book of prophecy. It tells what will happen at the end of time. What is the name of this last book in the Bible?_____

⭐

Beginnings

Where Are We?

Genesis 1-11

What Is the Big Picture?

Genesis was written by Moses. This section of the book tells how God created everything, including a plan for salvation after people sinned against Him. Genesis means "beginnings."

Who Are the Main Players?

Adam and Eve; Cain and Abel; and Noah and his family.

Digging In

Read chapter 1 and write the order in which God created the world.

Day 1:_____

Day 2:_____

Day 3:_____

Day 4:_____

Day 5:_____

Day 6:_____

Read verse 27. In whose image are people made?

_____

Read chapter 2, verses 1-3. What did God do on the seventh day?

_____

Read 2:18. Why did God create women?

_____

Read Genesis 3 to find out how sin came into the world.
Write out the story in your own words.

_____

_____

_____

_____

_____

Digging deeper

Read about Cain and Abel in chapter 4.
Read about a man who didn't die in 5:21-24.
Read about the oldest man in the Bible in 5:25-27.
Read chapter 11 and discover what happened when people
tried to build a tower to heaven.

Plant God's Word

In the beginning God created the heavens and the earth.
— Genesis 1:1

*So God created man in his own image, in the image of God he created
him; male and female he created them.*
— Genesis 1:27

*I will remember my covenant between me and you and all living
creatures of every kind. Never again will the waters become a flood to
destroy all life.*
— Genesis 9:15

⭐

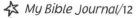
Father of Nations

Where Are We?

Genesis 12-23

What's Happening?

Events in the life of Abraham, a godly man

What Is the Big Picture?

Genesis was written by Moses. This section tells about how Abraham allowed God to lead him throughout his life.

Who Are the Main Players?

Abraham, Sarah and Lot

Digging In

Read chapter 12: 1-5. What did God call Abram to do?

_____

_____

What did God promise Abram in verses 12:2-3?

_____

_____

Who went with Abram? (12:4-5)

_____

Read chapter 13. Why did Abram and Lot separate?

_____

What was God's promise to Abraham in 17:16? Read verse 17 to find out why that was so unbelievable to Abraham.

_____

Read 21:1-7. What gift did God give to Abraham and Sarah?

_____

Digging Deeper

Read chapter 16 about Ishmael. Think about how God took care of Ishmael and how He takes care of you.

Read chapters 18 and 19 about Sodom and Gomorrah. What kind of warning is Lot's wife an example of?

Plant God's Word

I will establish my covenant as an everlasting covenant between me and you and your descendants after you for the generations to come, to be your God and the God of your descendants after you.
— Genesis 17:7

Blessings and Dreams

Where Are We?

Genesis 24-33

What Is the Big Picture?

Genesis was written by Moses. God used Isaac and Jacob in the leading and guidance of His people.

Who Are the Main Players?

Isaac, Rebekah, Jacob and Esau

Digging In

Read chapter 24 to find how Isaac got his wife. What was her name?

_____

Read 25:19-34. Who were the twins? Who were their parents? What did one twin do to receive something that belonged to the other?

_____

_____

Read chapter 27 to find out about a blessing given to the wrong son. Who helped one son get the blessing instead of his brother?

_____

_____

⭐

Read 28:10-22. What dream did Jacob have? What did Jacob promise to give God if God took care of him? (28:20-22)

_____

_____

Read chapter 29 and write how Jacob ended up with two wives who were sisters. What were their names?

_____

_____

Digging Deeper

Read chapter 30:1-24 to find out about Jacob's children. Who was Rachel's firstborn son?

_____

Read 30:25-43 to see how Jacob tricked Laban, Rachel and Leah's father.

Read chapters 32&33 to discover two important stories: 1. Jacob and Esau meet again. 2. Jacob wrestles with God.

Plant God's Word

I am with you and will watch over you wherever you go, and I will bring you back to this land. I will not leave you until I have done what I have promised you.

— Genesis 28:15

Joseph the Dreamer

Where Are We?

Genesis 34-41

What Is the Big Picture?

Genesis was written by Moses. This section of Genesis tells about Joseph — how he ended up in Egypt, and how God kept him safe and used him for His glory. There is going to be a great famine in the land.

Who Are the Main Players?

Jacob, Joseph and Joseph's brothers

Digging In

Read chapter 37 about Joseph and his brothers. Why were they jealous of Joseph?

_____

_____

What did Joseph dream about?

_____

What did his brothers do to him?

_____

What did they tell Jacob about his son, Joseph?

_____

_____

Read chapter 39 and find who told a lie that caused Joseph to be put into prison.

_____

_____

Read chapter 41 to find out about Pharaoh's dreams. Who told him what the dreams meant?

_____

How many years of abundance would there be? How many years of famine would follow?

_____

Who did Pharaoh put in charge of storing up food before the famine?

_____

Digging Deeper

Read 35:23-26 to find the names of Jacob's twelve sons.

Read all of chapter 40 to find out about the cupbearer and the baker in prison.

Read 41:41-43 to find out what Pharaoh gave to Joseph.

Plant God's Word

But while Joseph was there in the prison, the Lord was with him.
— Genesis 39:20-21

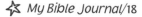
Used by God

Where Are We?

Genesis 42-50

What Is the Big Picture?

God allowed Joseph to be taken away from his home in earlier
chapters. He kept Joseph in His care while waiting to
use him in a special way. In these chapters, Joseph is able to
help his own family, as well as countless families in Egypt.
The stored food and grain kept families from starving during
the seven years of famine. All that happened to Joseph was
in God's plan — His own "big picture."

Who Are the Main Players?

Joseph, his brothers and his father, Jacob

Digging In

Read 42:1-3 to find out why Joseph's brothers went to Egypt. In
verse 1, what were the brothers doing?

_____

Read 42:4-5. Did all of Joseph's brothers go to Egypt? Why or
why not?

_____

_____

Read 42:6-38. How did Joseph get to teach his brothers a
lesson?

_____

_____

In chapter 44, what trick did Joseph play on his brothers?

_____

_____

Read chapter 45:1-8 about Joseph's reunion with his brothers. In verse 8, what does he tell his brothers?

_____

_____

In chapter 46, Israel is the same as Jacob (God gave him that name in chapter 32:28). In verse 7, who went to Egypt with Jacob?

_____

In 47:11, find out where Joseph's family settled. Read verses 13-31 to find out why the people came into bondage.

Digging Deeper

Read 42:24 and 29-30. Find out how Joseph felt about his brothers. Did he really want to hurt them?

_____

_____

Read 48:10-22 about a mixed-up blessing for Joseph's sons.

Read 50:19-21 about forgiveness for Joseph's brothers.

Plant God's Word

"I am God, the God of your father," he said. "Do not be afraid to go down to Egypt, for I will make you into a great nation there."
— Genesis 46:3

⭐

Moses, God's Leader

Where Are We?

Exodus 1-11

What Is the Big Picture?

Exodus was written by Moses. God's people became enslaved in Egypt (Genesis 47 tells how). Chapter 1 of Exodus tells how the Egyptians became meaner to the Israelites in Egypt. This section of Exodus tells how God begins to deal with Pharaoh to free His people. Exodus is called "the book of departure from Egypt." Exodus means "going out."

Who Are the Main Players?

Moses, Aaron, Miriam and Pharaoh

Digging In

Read chapter 1 to find out how God's people became oppressed.

Read chapter 2 to find out about Moses' birth and why he had to leave his home. Write the reason here. _____

_____

_____

Read about Moses and the burning bush in chapter 3. Write verse 5 here.

_____

_____

☆

Read chapter 5 to find out how God begins to deal with Pharaoh. Why did Pharaoh order the Israelites to make bricks without straw?

_____

How did the people treat Moses and Aaron? (Read verse 21 to find out.)

_____

_____

Search though chapters 7-11 and write out the ten plagues here.

_____

_____

Digging Deeper

Read chapter 2:1-8. On a separate sheet of paper, draw a cartoon of this story.

Read chapter 4 to discover why God gave Moses signs. What did Moses not want to do? From whom did God tell Moses to get help?

_____

_____

Plant God's Word

God said to Moses, "I am who I am. This is what you are to say to the Israelites: 'I am has sent me to you.'"

— Exodus 3:14

I have raised you up for this very purpose, that I might show you my power and that my name might be proclaimed in all the earth.

— Exodus 9:16

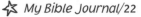

The Escape and the Wilderness

Where Are We?

Exodus 12-18

What Is the Big Picture?

Exodus was written by Moses. God helps His people escape from Egypt in this section. It is interesting to notice how quickly the Hebrews begin to grumble. They say many times that it would be better to be back in Egypt where they were treated badly than to have the current trouble. God is very patient in dealing with His grumbling people.

Who Are the Main Players?

Moses, Aaron and Pharaoh

Digging In

Read Chapter 12:1-20. What was going to happen on Passover night? (12:12-13).

_____

What were God's people to put on their door frames? (12:22-23)

_____

In chapter 16, what were the people complaining about?

_____

How did God provide? _____

_____

In chapter 17, the people began to complain again. What were they complaining about this time?

Moses became a judge for the people in chapter 18. What did his father-in-law, Jethro, suggest? (18:14-23)

Digging Deeper

How did God guide the people? (13:21-22)

In 17:8-15, who attacked the Israelites? Who did Moses send out to fight against them? (17:9-10)

Verses 11-13 tell how Joshua defeated the Amalekites. What did Moses have to do during the entire battle?

Read chapter 15:22-27. How did Moses make the water sweet in verse 25?

Plant God's Word

All the Israelites did just what the Lord had commanded Moses and Aaron. And on that very day the Lord brought the Israelites out of Egypt by their divisions.
— Exodus 12:50-51

The Lord is my strength and my song; he has become my salvation. He is my God, and I will praise him, my father's God, and I will exalt him.
— Exodus 15:2

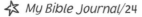

God's Laws

Where Are We?

Exodus 19-31

What Is the Big Picture?

Exodus was written by Moses. God is ready to begin leading His people to become a great nation. God has chosen the Israelites as His special people. The only thing they have to do to be God's special people is to follow His ways — obey His laws.

Who Are the Main Players?

Moses and Aaron

Digging In

Read chapter 19 to found out what happened at Mount Sinai.

What would happen to anyone who touched the mountain while God was on it? (19:12)

_____

In chapter 20, read and write out the ten commandments.

_____

_____

_____

_____

_____

_____

_____

What did the people think would happen if God spoke directly to them instead of using Moses? (20:19)

Read chapter 24 to see how God made His covenant with the people.

Chapter 31:1-11 tells that God gave each person the skills to serve Him in the way He appointed.

What did God give Moses in 31:18?

Digging Deeper

Read chapters 20-23 and write out some laws that God gave.

Read through chapters 25-30 to find rules about making a tabernacle and worshipping God.(*Hint. If your Bible has sub-headings, skim through to get the main idea of the chapters. Go back later and read the whole chapter, or choose a little to read each day.*)

Plant God's Word

Now if you obey me fully and keep my covenant, then out of all nations you will be my treasured possession. Although the whole earth is mine, you will be for me a kingdom of priests and a holy nation.

— Exodus 19:5-6

You shall have no other gods before me.

— Exodus 20:3

Remember the Sabbath day by keeping it holy.

— Exodus 20:8

⭐

A Golden Calf and a Place of Worship

Where Are We?

Exodus 32-40

What Is the Big Picture?

God has given His commandments. He is now ready for His people to begin their journey to the Promised Land. However, an impatient group of people anger God by making and worshipping an idol. God is very patient, although His wrath does burn against the people at times.

Who Are the Main Players?

Moses and Aaron

Digging In

In chapter 32, read about the people making a golden calf. Where was Moses? (32:1) _____

_____

Who told Moses about the golden calf? (32:7-8)

_____

_____

Who wrote on the tablets Moses carried? (32:15-16)

_____

What did Moses do with the tablets? (32:19)

_____

☆

What did he do with the golden calf? (32:20)

_____

_____

Why did the Levites kill many of God's people on that day?
(32:20-29)

_____

_____

_____

Digging Deeper

How did the people get new stone tablets?
Read Exodus 34:1-28.

Read 34:29-35 to find out why Moses' face was radiant.

Most of the rest of the book of Exodus tells about the
construction of the Tabernacle. Read through it a few
verses at a time.

Plant God's Word

*The Lord replied, "My Presence will go with you, and I will give
you rest."*

— Exodus 33:14

*And the Lord said, "I will cause all my goodness to pass in front of
you, and I will proclaim my name, the Lord, in your presence. I will
have mercy on whom I will have mercy, and I will have compassion
on whom I will have compassion."*

— Exodus 33:19

⭐

Rules to Live By

Where Are We?

The book of Leviticus

What Is the Big Picture?

Leviticus was written by Moses. It is called the
book of atonement. It was given to the people as a
guidebook on how to live as a holy people.

Digging In

Chapters 1-10 show many offerings that the people were to
offer. This was to give the people atonement for sins. List at
least four kinds of offerings and explain them.

_____

_____

_____

Read chapter 8 about Aaron and his sons becoming priests.

Chapters 11-27 show the people how to be pure. List at least
four kinds of regulations about purity and explain them.

_____

_____

_____

Read chapter 26 to find the reward for obedience and the
punishment for disobedience.

Find where these celebrations and holy-days are listed and
read about them:

The Sabbath

The Passover and Feast of Unleavened Bread

Firstfruits

Feast of Weeks

Feast of Trumpets
Day of Atonement
Feast of Tabernacles
Sabbath Year
Year of Jubilee

Digging Deeper

Read chapter 10:1-5 to find why two of Aaron's sons were killed.

Find in 24:1-9 about oil for the lamps (verse 4 tells about the pure gold lampstand); and the bread for the priests (verse 9 tells where Aaron and his sons are to eat this bread).

Read chapter 24:10-23 and discover what happened to a blasphemer (one who cursed the name of God).

Plant the Word

"Speak to the entire assembly of Israel and say to them, 'Be holy because I, the Lord your God, am holy.'"

— Leviticus 19:2

⭐

Count Off and March!

Where Are We?

The book of Numbers

What Is the Big Picture?

Numbers was written by Moses. God is preparing His people for their wilderness journey, and also for their entrance into the Promised Land. The Israelites are numbered twice by census. The Tabernacle is set up and dedicated.

Digging In

Read chapter 1:1-4 to find God's instructions about counting the Israelites. Who was to be counted? (1:3)

_____

_____

In chapters 7-10:10, the tabernacle is set up. Many commands are in these chapters about the dedication of the Tabernacle. In 7:1, what did Moses do?

_____

_____

_____

In 7:2, what did the leaders of the nation do?

_____

_____

_____

In chapter 14, why did the people rebel?

⭐

_____

_____

_____

In chapter 22, the Moab people are worried about the Israelites taking over all their land. What did the king do for them? (22:6)

_____

_____

_____

Plant God's Word

I am the Lord your God, who brought you out of Egypt to be your God. I am the Lord your God.

— Numbers 15:41

☆

Reviewing Laws for a New Generation

Where Are We?

The book of Deuteronomy

What Is the Big Picture?

Deuteronomy was written by Moses. Moses reviews the events of the past years and the laws from God. A new generation of people have become adults and they need to be prepared to enter the Promised Land.

Digging In

Read 3:21-29 to find out why Moses will not enter the Promised Land. Who will be the new leader? (verse 28)

_____

Read in these chapters what God says about His people's relationship to Him. Write one sentence to describe each.

4:1-14 _____

4:32-40 _____

Chapter 6 _____

Chapter 8 _____

10:12-22 _____

Chapter 11 _____

✫

26:16-19 _____

Read about the renewal of God's covenant with His people in chapter 29:1-15.

Digging Deeper

What does chapter 4 tell about? (verse 4)

Can you pick out the review of the Ten Commandments in chapter 5? Find all ten.

Read 30:1-10 and write what God promises those who follow His ways.

_____

Plant God's Word

Love the Lord your God with all your heart and with all your soul and with all your strength. These commandments that I give you today are to be upon your hearts. Impress them on your children. Talk about them when you sit at home and when you walk along the road, when you lie down and when you get up. Tie them as symbols on your hands and bind them on your foreheads. Write them on the door frames of your houses and on your gates.

— Deuteronomy 6:5-9

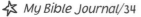

The Promised Land

Where Are We?

The book of Joshua

What Is the Big Picture?

Joshua wrote the book of Joshua. Moses has died.
God puts Joshua in charge of leading the Israelites. They
have reached the Promised Land. God's people will now
move into the land, defeat the ungodly people who live
there and settle in different parts of the land.

Who Are the Main Players?

Joshua, the Israelites and many kings

Digging In

Read Joshua 1:1-9 to see what God commanded Joshua to do.
What did God tell Joshua to have the people get ready to do?
(verse 2) _____

In chapter 3, what was unusual about the Israelites crossing the
Jordan River?_____

Read 5:13-6:25 about the fall of Jericho. How many times did
they march around the walls of Jericho each day for six days?
_____How many times on the seventh day?_____

In 8:30-35, God renews His covenant with the Israelites. What
did Joshua do in verse 32?_____What did Joshua do in
verses 34 and 35? _____

Read chapter 9 to find out which people tricked Joshua so he
would not go to battle against them. What was the trick?

_____

In chapter 10, five kings and their armies attacked Gibeon. What miracles happened so that Joshua's armies could defeat these five kings? (verses 11-15)

_____

Digging Deeper

Read Chapter 4:1-9. What did God have some of the men take from the middle of the Jordan River, and what did they do with these things?_____

Look in chapter 12 to find a list of all the kings that Joshua and the Israelites defeated.

Look up the following verses in the Bible and see where God promised the land flowing with milk and honey to His people many times. Write the names of the lands mentioned in some of the verses.

Exodus 3:8, 17; 13:5; 33:3_____

Leviticus 20:24 _____

Numbers 14:8 _____

Deuteronomy 6:3; 11:9; 26:9,15; 27:3._____

Plant God's Word

Now fear the Lord and serve him with all faithfulness. Throw away the gods your forefathers worshiped beyond the River and in Egypt, and serve the Lord. But if serving the Lord seems undesirable to you, then choose for yourselves this day whom you will serve, whether the gods your forefathers served beyond the River, or the gods of the Amorites, in whose land you are living. But as for me and my household, we will serve the Lord.

— Joshua 24:14-15

⭐

God Appoints Judges

Where Are We?

The book of Judges

What Is the Big Picture?

The writer of this book may have been Samuel. The Israelites disobeyed God by not driving out all the Canaanites. Then God's own people began to live like these ungodly ones. So God raised up judges to deliver His word, to deliver His people from the enemies and to rule over the people.

Who Are the Main Players?

Twelve judges including, Deborah, Gideon and Samson

Digging In

Read 2:1-4 about why God is angry with the Israelites.

Read 2:13-15. Write the names of two idols the people worshipped._____ What did God do to His people when they worshipped these idols?

_____

Read the story of Deborah in chapter 4. What was she called in verse 4?

_____

God told Deborah to send this man as leader of the army to Mount Tabor. What was his name? (verse 6)_____ Who did this man say must come with him? (verses 8-9)

_____

⭐

Chapters 6 and 7 tell about Gideon. Read all about him, then fill in the blanks below.

In 6:13, what question did Gideon ask about God?

_____

In 6:25-26, God ordered Gideon to tear down _____, and to build_____.

In 6:31, Joash said to the angry crowd, "If _____ is really a_____, he can defend himself."

Read 6:33-40. What did Gideon ask God to do with fleece?

_____

Read 7:1-8. How did God choose the army of 300?

_____

Plant God's Word

But Gideon told them, "I will not rule over you, nor will my son rule over you. The Lord will rule over you."

— Judges 8:23

Then Manoah prayed to the Lord: "O Lord, I beg you, let the man of God you sent to us come again to teach us how to bring up the boy who is to be born."

— Judges 13:8

Loyalty and Love

Where Are We?
The book of Ruth

What Is the Big Picture?
This book tells of loyalty. It was probably written by Samuel. Ruth is not a Jew, one of God's chosen people. Yet, she chooses to stay with Naomi and worship her God. Someone very special is born because of the marriage between Ruth and Boaz.

Who Are the Main Players?
Naomi, Ruth, Orpah and Boaz

Digging In

Read the entire book. It is only four chapters long.

In 1:1-2, where do you learn that Naomi was from? What caused her and her husband to leave their home?

_____

In 1:4, what do you learn was the group of people Ruth was from?

_____

In 1:6-7, why was Naomi going back to Judah?

_____

In 2:11-12, why did Boaz treat Ruth so well?

_____

In 3:12, why didn't Boaz marry Ruth right away?

☆

In 4:7-8, why did the man give Boaz his sandal?

In 4:10, read why it was important for Ruth to find someone who was related to her husband who died.

In 4:16, what did Ruth and Boaz name their son?

In 4:16 & 22, who was the special person who would be born in later generations? (He would become a king!)

Digging Deeper

Read Deuteronomy 25:5-10 to find God's rules about who widows should marry. These verses also contain the law about the sandal.

Read these verses to find Boaz and Obed in the family tree of Jesus: Matthew 1:5; Luke 3:32.

Plant God's Word

But Ruth replied, "Don't urge me to leave you or to turn back from you. Where you go I will go, and where you stay I will stay. Your people will be my people and your God my God."

— Ruth 1:16

Israel Becomes a Kingdom

Where Are We?

The book of 1 Samuel

What Is the Big Picture?

This book was probably written by Samuel through chapter 24. The rest could have been written by Nathan and Gad. The Israelites became tired of being ruled by judges and wanted to be like other nations. They wanted to have a king. God allowed this to happen. 1 Samuel tells of the last two judges, Eli and Samuel, and the first two kings, Saul and David.

Who Are the Main Players?

Eli, Hannah, Samuel, Saul, Jonathan, David and Goliath

Digging In

Read chapter 1. Who thought Hannah was drunk with wine when she was praying very hard?_____(verse 13-14) What was she praying for?_____ (verse 11)

In verses 21-28, where did Hannah take Samuel, and why?

_____

Read chapter 3. Who heard voices in the night? Who was speaking?_____

In 3:19-4:1, who began to speak for the Lord to all of Israel?

_____

Read about the ark of the covenant in chapter 4:3-6. What did the Israelites do when the ark arrived in the camp? (verse 5)

_____

⭐

Why were the Philistines afraid of the ark? (verses 7-9)

_____

What happened in verse 11?_____

In chapter 8, Israel demands a king. Who was still judge?
(verses 1-4)_____

Read how God responds in verses 19-22.

Who was chosen to be the next king in chapter 16:6-13?

_____

Why did Saul hate David? (18:7)

_____

Digging Deeper

Read 2:12-17 about Eli's sons. Did they respect God and His
laws?_____(verses 12 &17)

Read 7:12-14. What is the Ebenezer stone?_____

Read 18:20-22. Who did David marry?_____How did
she help him in 19:11-17?_____

In 20:35-42, who helped David escape Saul? _____

Whose life did David spare in 24:1-7 and 26:6-16?

_____

Plant God's Word

*But be sure to fear the Lord and serve him faithfully with all your
heart; consider what great things he has done for you.*
— 1 Samuel 12:24

*The Lord does not look at the things man looks at. Man looks at the
outward appearance, but the Lord looks at the heart.*
— 1 Samuel 16:7

✰

King David

Where Are We?

The book of 2 Samuel

What Is the Big Picture?

2 Samuel was probably compiled (put together as a book)
by Ezra or Jeremiah. Saul and his sons have died, and David
mourns greatly. David is now anointed king. This book tells of
David's reign as king. David is favored in the sight of God.
But David does some sinful things. He has to deal with his
own sins and repent to God. Note: In these books of the Old
Testament, there are a lot of battles, a lot of slayings, a lot of
people killed. There is a reason for all the killing. Those who
were killed were enemies of God. The nations that opposed
the Israelites did not worship our God. They worshipped
idols and did horrible things, such as sacrificing their
own children to false gods.

Who Are the Main Players?

David, Mephibosheth, Uriah, Bathsheba, Nathan and Solomon

Digging In

Read 5:17-25. Who did David's army defeat? _____

What did they capture to bring back home? (6:1-5)_____

Read 7:4-6. What is God asking David to build for Him?

_____

Read all of chapter 11. What sins did David commit?

_____

_____

In 12:1-7, Nathan told David a "story." Who was the story really about? (verse 7)

_____

In verse 24, David and Bathsheba have a second son. The first died because of David's sin. The second son is named _____. (The entire story of the birth of both sons is in 12:14-25.)

In chapter 24, David is given a choice by God. (verses 10-14) The punishment David chose was to have a plague for 3 days. He would rather have the plague in Israel than to have enemies killing his people. But in verses 18-25, the plague was stopped. What did David do to stop the plague?

_____

_____

Digging Deeper

Read 6:6-11. What happened when someone stumbled and accidentally touched the ark? _____

Who was this person? _____

Where was the ark placed when David was afraid to take it into the city? _____

Read chapter 9 about Mephibosheth. Whose son was he? Why did David treat him well? _____

Plant God's Word

The Lord is my rock, my fortress and my deliverer.

— 2 Samuel 22:2

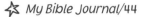

A Wise King

Where Are We?
The book of 1 Kings

What Is the Big Picture?
It is uncertain who wrote this book. It may have been
Ezra or Jeremiah who put together the recorded events to write
the book. 1 Kings tells about the reign of Solomon, the building
of God's temple and the building of Solomon's palace.
Then it goes on to tell of Elijah, the prophet, and of other
kings who reigned over God's people.

Who Are the Main Players?
David, Solomon and Elijah

Digging In

Read chapter 1 about Adonijah. What did he want to do? (verse
5)

_____

In verse 12, why was Nathan the prophet worried about
Bathsheba and Solomon? _____

Read verses 12-53. Who became king? _____
What happened to Adonijah in 2:13-15?_____

Read all of chapter 3. What did Solomon ask God
for?_____Why did God tell Solomon he could have
anything he wanted?_____ (verse 6)

Read 6:11-13. What did God promise Solomon? _____

In chapter 8, what important item was brought to the temple?
(verse 6)_____ Which of God's laws was Solomon
breaking in chapter 11? (verses 1-2)_____

What did these wives cause Solomon to do? _____
(verses 4-8)

What warning did God give to Solomon in verses 9-13?

_____

Chapter 19:9-18 tells of Elijah's meeting with God in a mountain cave. In verse 18, how many people of Israel will God spare? What did these people not do to anger God?

_____

Read verses 19-21. What did Elijah cast onto Elisha?

_____

Digging Deeper

Read 5:3-5 again. Now go back to 2 Samuel 7:5-6 and read where God asked David to build him a temple.

Read chapter 9:1-9, God's covenant with Solomon. What would God do if the people and Solomon stopped obeying Him and started worshipping false gods and idols?_____
(verses 6-8)

In 10:1-13, what Queen came to visit Solomon?

_____

Read 19:1-8 about Elijah and Jezebel.

Plant God's Word

Observe what the Lord your God requires: Walk in his ways, and keep his decrees and commands, his laws and requirements, as written in the Law of Moses, so that you may prosper in all you do and wherever you go.

— 1 Kings 2:3

⭐

God's People Taken Captive

Where Are We?

The book of 2 Kings

What Is the Big Picture?

It is not known who wrote 2 Kings. In this book, God's people come under the rule of several kings and are led into sin again and again. God sends His word through prophets. Much of God's Word is a call to repentance and a warning for punishment. God's people are taken captive because of their continuous sinning against God.

Who Are the Main Players?

Elijah, Elisha, Isaiah and several kings

Digging In

In chapter 1, King Ahaziah of Israel was injured. He sent his men to ask a false god, Baalzebub, a god in Ekron, whether he would get well or die. Who did God send to stop the men from seeking a false god? (verse 3) _____

What was the message from God that this man delivered? (verse 4) _____

In verses 13-15, what did the captain of the third group of 50 men ask Elijah? _____

What happened to Ahaziah in verse 17? _____

Read chapter 2:1-12. What happened to Elijah? If Elisha saw Elijah leave this earth, what did that mean? (verses 9-10)

_____

_____

⭐

Read chapter 4 about the widow's jar of oil, Elisha raising a dead son, poisonous food made harmless, and the feeding of the hundred men. Who did these miracles for God?

_____

In 11:21, how old was Joash when he became king of Judah?_____ Who was this king's helper? (12:2)_____ In verse 4, what did Joash begin to repair?_____

2 Kings 18:9-12 and 25:1-6 tell of God's people being taken captive. Why did God allow this? (verse 18:12)_____

Who began speaking as prophet of God in 19:2?_____

Digging Deeper

In chapter 5:1-14, who had leprosy?_____ How was he cured?_____

In 5:15-27, who was greedy? What was his punishment?

_____

Read in 6:8-7:20 about the Syrians. Tell three things about them. _____

_____

_____

_____

Plant God's Word

As they were walking along and talking together, suddenly a chariot of fire and horses of fire appeared and separated the two of them, and Elijah went up to heaven in a whirlwind.

— 2 Kings 2:11

David

Where Are We?

The book of 1 Chronicles

What Is the Big Picture?

1 Chronicles was probably written or compiled by Ezra.
1 Chronicles begins as a family tree record beginning from
Adam. This book was written as a historical record of the
events of the Israelites under the reign of King David. Much
of what you will read is repeated from 1 & 2 Samuel and 1 &
2 Kings. This is so that the people returning from captivity in
Babylon would know the history of their people.

Who Are the Main Players?

David and God's people

Digging In

In chapter 9, we are told that Judah was taken captive by the
Babylonian people because of_____. (verse 1)

David's family and his reign as king are described beginning in
chapter 11. What does 11:9 say about David?_____

_____

In chapter 13, the story of moving the ark is repeated. What
is the name of the man who died because he touched the ark?
(verses 9-10)_____

Read chapter 16. What were the people celebrating?

_____

In chapter 21, who caused David to take a census? (verse 1)

_____

What was God's punishment for this act? _____
(verse 14)

In verse 30, what was David afraid of? _____

What did David prepare to build in chapter 22? _____

Digging Deeper

1 Chronicles 16:1-36 is a psalm of David. David wrote many of
the chapters in the book of Psalms. Read this psalm and write
down at least four praise words that David used to praise God.

_____

_____

_____

Plant God's Word

*Give thanks to the Lord, call on his name; make known among the
nations what he has done. Sing to him, sing praise to him; tell of all
his wonderful acts. Glory in his holy name; let the hearts of those who
seek the Lord rejoice!*

— 1 Chronicles 16:8-10

⭐

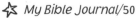

Solomon

Where Are We?

The book of 2 Chronicles

What Is the Big Picture?

2 Chronicles was probably written from records compiled by Ezra. Much of the writing in this book is repeated from 1 & 2 Kings. The Chronicles were written to provide a chronological (in order) record of the history of God's people.

Who Are the Main Players?

Solomon and other kings

Digging In

Chapter 1 tells about the greatness of _____. (verse 1)
Who was with him? _____

Chapters 2-5 tell of building the temple. In 5:2, what did Solomon want to bring to the temple? _____

In 7:1-3, what filled the temple? _____

In 7:15, what will God hear? _____

In 7:17-18, what was God's promise to Solomon? _____

Read 12:1-4 to find out God's punishment against Rehoboam and the people for not following God's laws.

Digging Deeper

Read a little about each of these good kings in 2 Chronicles.

Asa — 14:1-4

Jehoshaphat — 17:3-5

Joash — 24:1-2

Amaziah — 25:1-2

Uzziah — 26:3-5

Jotham — 27:1-2

Hezekiah — 29:1-2

Josiah — 34:1-3

Plant God's Word

Have faith in the Lord your God and you will be upheld; have faith in his prophets and you will be successful.

— 2 Chronicles 20:20

☆

God's Returning People

Where Are We?

The book of Ezra

What Is the Big Picture?

It was probably Ezra who wrote this book. Ezra tells the
fulfillment of prophecy about God's people returning from
captivity. This book also tells about Ezra, who was
devoted to studying God's Word.

Who Are the Main Players?

Ezra, Zerubbabel and God's people

Digging In

Which king made a proclamation to let God's people go to
Jerusalem and rebuild the temple? (1:1)

_____

In 2:68-69, what did the people give?

_____

What did they rebuild first? (7:1-7)

_____

In chapter 4, enemies of God's people tried to stop the
rebuilding of the temple. In verse 12, what is the city
called?_____ In verses 23-24 what did the enemies
make the builders do?_____

Read 7:1-6. What was Ezra skilled in? (verse 6)

_____

☆ Whose hand was on Ezra? (verse 6)

_____

In 7:11-28, another king, Artaxerxes, gives more of God's people their freedom to go to Jerusalem. Gold, silver, and other valuables are also sent along, to help rebuild God's house. Artaxerxes was also told to appoint _____ and _____. (verse 25)

What did Ezra have the people do in 8:21?

_____

_____

What did Ezra say about the people's sins in 9:6?

_____

_____

Digging Deeper

Read 6:13-22 about the rebuilding and dedication of the temple.

Read all of chapter 10 about foreign wives.

Plant God's Word

He is good; his love to Israel endures forever.

— Ezra 3:11

Returning People and a Restored City

Where Are We?

The book of Nehemiah

What Is the Big Picture?

This book was written by Nehemiah. More people return from captivity. The walls around Jerusalem are built. With this book, the history of the Old Testament is finished. The history of God's people has been told. All the rest of the Old Testament books fit within the time up to the writing of Nehemiah.

Who Are the Main Players?

Nehemiah and God's people

Digging In

In 1:11-2:1, what was Nehemiah to the king?

_____

In 2:17-20, what did Nehemiah want to have done?

_____

In 4:1-3, who were the two men ridiculing God's people for rebuilding the walls? _____

What were the false rumors about Nehemiah in chapter 6? (verses 6-7)_____

Read 8:5-8. Who read the law to the people? _____
In verse 9, who is the governor? Who is the priest?

_____

What did the people do in 9:1-2? What did they do for a quarter of the day? Then for another quarter? (verse 3)

In 13:1-3, who was separated from Israel?

Digging Deeper

What were Hanani and Hananiah appointed to do? (7:1-3)

In chapter 9:26-28, what did the people begin to do?

Plant God's Word

Stand up and praise the Lord your God, who is from everlasting to everlasting. Blessed be your glorious name, and may it be exalted above all blessing and praise.

— Nehemiah 9:5

☆

The Queen Who Saved Her People

Where Are We?

The book of Esther

What Is the Big Picture?

Esther was probably written by Mordecai. God put Esther where she could help save His people. His people, called Jews, were hated by many, mainly because they refused to worship people and false gods. Those who were not Jews were called Gentiles. Esther was a Jewish woman and she married a Gentile, the king. This was all in God's plan to save His people. Mordecai was Esther's cousin, but he adopted her when her parents died.

Who Are the Main Players?

King Ahasuerus, Queen Vashti, Esther, Mordecai and Haman

Digging In

Read 1:1-4 to find out about King Ahasuerus' riches and the banquet he held. What did Queen Vashti refuse to do in verses 10-12?_____ What happened to Vashti?_____ (verse 19) What was the king searching for in 2:4?_____

Why did she not tell the king and his servants she was a Jew? (2:10)_____

What did Haman want to do to all Jews? (3:5-6)_____

Read chapter 4 to find out how Esther helps save her people. In verses 11-12, what is Esther afraid of? _____

Read chapters 5-9 to discover the story of how Esther saved her people and what happened to Haman who wanted to destroy the Jews.

Digging Deeper

Read 2:19-23. Who was planning to kill the king? Who saved the king's life by telling Esther about the plan?_____

_____

How did the events in 2:19-23 help save Mordecai's life in 6:1-14?_____

Read 8:1-2. Who was promoted in Haman's place?

_____

What feast was begun by the Jews after these events?(9:26)

_____

Read 9:20 to find out why Mordecai probably wrote this book.

Plant God's Word

And who knows but that you have come to royal position for such as time as this?

— Esther 4:14

A Man Tested

Where Are We?

The book of Job

What is the Big Picture?

The book was probably written by Job, but other possibilities
are Elihu or Moses. Job does ask why he did not just die.
But he does not curse God, as Satan would like. God carries Job
through all his troubles, and blesses him greatly in the end.

Who Are the Main Players?

Job, his wife and three friends (Eliphaz, Bildad, and Zophar),
also God and Satan

Digging In

Read about Job in 1:1. What kind of man was he?

_____

Read 1:13-22. Write out verse 22 here.

_____

In 2:1-6, God allowed Satan to touch Job and make him ill and
miserable. In verse 6, what was Satan supposed to spare?

_____

Read 2:7-8 to see what Satan did with Job. What did Job's
wife say in verses 9-10?_____ Read verse 10b and
compare it to the verse you wrote out above.

Verses 2:11-13 tells about Job's three friends coming to visit
him. Why did they not speak to him?_____
(verse 13b)

In chapter 3, Job curses the day he was born. In chapter 6 he wants God to let him die. In chapter 7, Job calls out to God. In chapter 9, Job defends God. In chapter 10, Job acknowledges that God is creator.

In chapter 19:25-29, Job proclaims his faith in God, the redeemer.

In chapter 32-37, Elihu speaks out for God.

In chapter 38, God speaks out of a whirlwind to tell Job that his Lord is in control of everything.

In chapter 40, Job answers God.

In chapter 42, Job repents. God gives Job back twice as much as he had before.

Digging Deeper

Read some of the arguments of Job's friends

Chapter 5:1-7 — Man is born to trouble.

Chapter 11:1-6 — Job must be full of guilt.

Chapter 11:13-20 — Job is told to repent of his sins.

Chapter 18:1-21 — The wicked are doomed to misery.

Plant God's Word

"Have you considered my servant Job? There is no one on earth like him; he is blameless and upright, a man who fears God and shuns evil."

— Job 1:8

✮

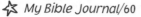
Express Yourself

Where Are We?

The book of Psalms

What is the Big Picture?

Psalms was written mostly by David. However, Moses,
Asaph, Solomon, Ethan, the sons of Korah and some
unknown writers also wrote parts of the book. Psalms is the
longest book in the Bible with 150 chapters.

Digging In

Read the following Psalms. A topic is listed with each reference
to give you an idea of the many kinds of verses in this book.
Write a word or two on the line below each listed psalm that
will you remind you about it.

Happiness: Psalm 1

_____

God's glory: Psalm 24

_____

Help, guidance, protection: Psalm 25-26

_____

Being righteous: Psalm 37

_____

Repentance: Psalm 51

_____

Punishment for the wicked: Psalm 58

_____

Salvation: Psalm 68:19-23

About Jesus: Psalm 110

Praise: Psalm 111

Digging Deeper

Memorize Psalm 105.

Read 104, 106, 108, 113, 138, 139.

Plant God's Word

Your word is a lamp to my feet and a light for my path.
— Psalm 119:105

Let everything that has breath praise the Lord. Praise the Lord.
— Psalm 150:6

A Book of Wise Sayings

Where Are We?

The book of Proverbs

What Is the Big Picture?

This book was written partly by Solomon.
Others also wrote some of the proverbs.
The main focus of the book is wisdom.

Digging In

Read 1:1-2. Why did Solomon write Proverbs?

_____

_____

_____

In 1:7, what is the beginning of knowledge?

_____

_____

_____

Read the following proverbs about these topics:

14:17 — A quick temper

23:13-14 — Disciplining a child

11:13 — Gossiping

10:23 — Foolish behavior

17:17 — Friendship

17:14 — Quarreling

10:12 — Hatred

21:23 — The tongue

Digging Deeper

Go back to 1 Kings 4:32. How many proverbs did Solomon write?

Read all of chapter 4 about wisdom. Write verse 27 here.

_____

_____

_____

_____

_____

Plant God's Word

Trust in the Lord with all your heart and lean not on your own understanding; in all your ways acknowledge him, and he will make your paths straight.

— Proverbs 3:5-6

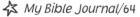

Happiness Is Obeying God

Where Are We?

The book of Ecclesiastes

What Is the Big Picture?

Solomon wrote this book. (Look at 1:1) This book was written to tell what life is like without God. For awhile, Solomon got away from God in his life. He wrote to tell others that life without God is meaningless.

Who Is the Main Player?

Solomon

Digging In

Read chapter 1. It seems depressing, doesn't it? That is because Solomon is telling what life is like when we are not living for God.

Read verses 16-18. Who does he think has more wisdom than anyone?_____ Does it do him any good to be wise and still not follow God?_____

Verse 17 is saying it is just like chasing the _____.

Read chapter 3:1-8. Who do you think judges when the time is right for all these things?

_____

_____

Read chapter 5:1-7. Write 7 here.

_____

_____

Read chapter 7 about wisdom. Write 7:13 here.

_____

_____

_____

Digging Deeper

Read chapter 11:1-6 These verses are often used in churches before offering is taken. Write out what at least one of the verses means in your own words.

_____

_____

_____

_____

_____

Plant God's Word

Fear God and keep his commandments, for this is the whole duty of man. For God will bring every deed into judgment, including every hidden thing, whether it is good or evil.

— Ecclesiastes 12:13-14

⭐

A Love Story

Where Are We?

The book of Song of Songs (or "Song of Solomon")

What Is the Big Picture?

Song of Songs was written by Solomon. This book is written as a love story. Solomon speaks of his lover and how beautiful she is. He speaks of how he longs for her beauty. Many of the writings in the Bible use symbolism (one thing means quite another).The writings in this book symbolize the love we should have for God and how He loves us back.

Digging In

Read this whole book. It only has seven chapters. Write some things in the book that might symbolize God's love for you.

_____

_____

_____

_____

Write some things that might symbolize your love for God.

_____

_____

_____

_____

_____

Digging Deeper

Look at verse 1:1 to show who wrote this book.

Plant God's Word

Imagine God's name in this verse to make a praise to him:
All beautiful you are, my darling [my Lord], there is no flaw in you.
— Song of Songs 4:7

⭐

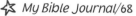

A Prophecy of Salvation

Where Are We?

The book of Isaiah

What Is the Big Picture?

Isaiah is the beginning of the books of Prophecy.
Prophets delivered God's Word to the people. Note: Most
of the prophets prophesied (gave God's Word) before Israel's
captivity in Babylon. Ezekiel and Daniel prophesied during
captivity. Haggai, Zechariah and Malachi prophesied after
the captivity. The book of Isaiah contains a lot of
prophecy about the coming of a Savior.

Digging In

Read chapter 1 about the vision Isaiah saw. What kind of
nation is God's people? (verses 2b and 4a)

_____

_____

Read verse 15 to find what God will do if the people pray to Him.

In 4:1, what words symbolize Jesus? _____

In 6:8-9, Isaiah says he will go and speak for the Lord.

Read 9:1-7. Who is this set of verses speaking about?

_____

Chapters 13-23 tell of predictions against foreign nations. Write
the names of at least three nations here.

_____

_____

Chapter 40 tells of _____ for God's people. (verse 1)

In chapter 47, Babylon falls and God's people are freed. What does God call Himself in verse 12? _____

Digging Deeper

Read 40:31 and write it here.

_____

_____

Read 66:4 where God's land will now be called Beulah Land.

Plant God's Word

For to us a child is born, to us a son is given, and the government will be on his shoulders. And he will be called Wonderful Counselor, Mighty God, Everlasting Father, Prince of Peace.

—Isaiah 9:6

The grass withers and the flowers fall, but the word of our God stands forever.

—Isaiah 40:8

⭐

The Weeping Prophet

Where Are We?

The book of Jeremiah

What Is the Big Picture?

Jeremiah lived in Jerusalem before and during the
invasion and captivity. Jeremiah called for God's people
to repent and stop sinning. He delivered God's Word
as the people continued to reject God and were
defeated and captured.

Digging In

In chapter 1:1-5, God calls Jeremiah to be a prophet. When did
God set Jeremiah apart to be a prophet? (verse 5)

_____

_____

In 2:5, what did God's people follow?_____

_____

In 2:9, who will God bring charges against?_____

_____

In 5:1, under what condition will God forgive this city?

_____

Look up each of Jeremiah's sufferings:

Plotted against — 11:18-21

Face to face with false prophets — 14:13-16 and 28:10-17

Persecuted — 15:10-18

⭐

Beaten and put into stocks — 20:1-2

Life was threatened — 26:8

Arrested — 36:26

Put into prison — 32:2-3

Some of his prophecies burned — 36:22-25

Put into a cistern — 38:6

Bound with chains — 40:1

Digging Deeper

Read parts of each chapter listed below to find out God's Word about these nations:

46 — Egypt

47 — Philistines

48 — Moab

49 — Ammon, Edom, Damascus, Kedar, Hazor, Elam

50 — Babylon

Plant God's Word

In those days and at that time I will make a righteous Branch sprout from David's line; he will do what is just and right in the land.

— Jeremiah 33:15

Mourning and Sorrow

Where Are We?

The book of Lamentations

What Is the Big Picture?

Lamentations was written by Jeremiah.
The interesting thing about this book is that it was written
in a type of poem. The original was written in the Hebrew
language. Jeremiah is filled with sorrow for Jerusalem.

Who Are the Main Players?

Jeremiah and God's nation of people

Digging In

Read this entire book.

In 1:11, what do people search for?

_____

In 2:1, what has God covered the nation with?

_____

3:25 tells that the Lord is good to _____.

4:22 says that God's _____ will end. But
_____ will always be punished.

What is gone from the hearts of those who do not obey God?
(5:15)_____

_____

✫

Digging Deeper

Read chapter 3 again. List some of the troubles that have come upon Jeremiah. _____

Remember that God had things happen to prophets as a symbol of the troubles that would come upon God's nation of sinful people. In the end, however, God blesses His prophets and His repentant people.

Plant God's Word

You, O Lord, reign forever; your throne endures from generation to generation.

— Lamentations 5:1

☆

Glory

Where Are We?

The book of Ezekiel

What Is the Big Picture?

Ezekiel wrote this book. Ezekiel prophesies about a sinful nation. He was one of the captives in Babylon. He tells of the glory of God and the lost glory of those who sin against God. But this book offers hope to God's people. Through all the sinfulness and rejection of their Lord, these people are saved. God gives glory back to His people when they repent.

Who Are the Main Players?

Ezekiel and God's people

Digging In

Read chapter 1 about Ezekiel's vision. Write verse 28 here:

_____

_____

Read chapter 2 about Ezekiel's call from God to give God's Word to the people.

In 2:9-3:3, what did God have Ezekiel do?

_____

_____

In chapter 10, the glory of the Lord leaves His people. Read verses 18-19.

⭐

Read chapter 37:1-14 about the Valley of Dry Bones.

Write out 48:35 here:

_____

_____

Digging Deeper

Read some parables from God:

Chapter 15 — A useless vine

Chapter 18 — Two eagles and a vine

Read prophecies against sinful nations, God's enemies:

Chapter 25, Ammon, Moab, Edom, Philistia

Chapter 26-28, Tyre

Chapter 29, Egypt

Chapter 38, Gog

Plant God's Word

*I will take you out of the nations; I will gather you from all the
countries and bring you back into your own land.*

— Ezekiel 36:24

*And I will put my Spirit in you and move you to follow my decrees
and be careful to keep my laws.*

— Ezekiel 36:27

⭐

Four Who Obeyed God

Where Are We?

The book of Daniel

What Is the Big Picture?

Daniel wrote this book. Daniel was a
prophet of dreams and visions. This book takes place while
God's people are captives in Babylon. The four young men
mentioned in the book of Daniel are among the first of the
captives to be taken to Babylon.

Who Are the Main Players?

Shadrach, Meshach, Abednego, Daniel,
King Nebuchadnezzar, King Belshazzar and King Darius

Digging In

Read the four main stories in this book:

In 1:8-16, Daniel and his friends are tempted with rich foods.
How many days did Daniel say to test them? (verse 12)

_____

In chapter 3, three men are in the fiery furnace. Why was the
king angry? (verse 12)

_____

In chapter 5 there is handwriting on the wall. What did the
king do for Daniel? (verse 29)

_____

In chapter 6, Daniel is in the lions's den.

Digging Deeper

Read about Daniel's visions:

Chapter 7 — Four beasts

Chapter 8 — A ram and a goat

Chapter 10 — A man

Planting God's Word

How great are his signs, how mighty his wonders! His kingdom is an eternal kingdom; his dominion endures from generation to generation.

— Daniel 4:3

Unfaithful

Where Are We?

The book of Hosea

What Is the Big Picture?

Hosea wrote this book. The book was written just before
the fall of Israel. It pictures God's living forgiveness of Israel
and how they pleaded for repentance.

Who Are the Main Players?

Hosea, his wife and the Israelites

Digging In

Read 1:2-3. What did God tell Hosea to do?

_____

Write out what God says about Israel loving other gods. (3:1)

_____

In 4:1-2, what is God's charge against His people?

_____

In 4:19, what is God going to send?

_____

Chapter 14 tells of the blessing that God has waiting for His

people, if they will only ask God to _____. (verse 2)

★

Digging Deeper

Read chapter 7 to find some of the sins that Israel committed.

_____

_____

_____

Read chapter 8 to find what punishments God will bring to His sinful people.

_____

_____

_____

Plant God's Word

The ways of the Lord are right; the righteous walk in them, but the rebellious stumble in them.

— Hosea 14:9

☆

Locusts

Where Are We?

The book of Joel

What Is the Big Picture?

This book was written by Joel. This short book was written
before Hosea. It is warning God's people of the destruction
that will be caused by their unfaithfulness to God.

Who Are the Main Players?

Joel and God's people

Digging In

Read the entire book. What is God going to send to destroy the
nation? (verse 4) _____

What does God call the people in verse 5? _____

In 2:13, what does God say about Himself? _____

In chapter 3, the nations are judged. In 3:17-21, God's blessing
are foretold.

What does God promise to do in 3:21? _____

Digging Deeper

In 1:3, who are the people commanded to tell of these things?

_____

In 2:11, what is the day of the Lord like?

_____

Read 3:9-11. Write how the people are to prepare for war.

_____

Write out 3:16b here:

_____

_____

_____

_____

_____

Plant God's Word

Then you will know that I [am]… God.

— Joel 3:17

The Plumb Line

Where Are We?

The book of Amos

What Is the Big Picture?

Amos wrote this book. The people were sinning so badly that they were at the point of no return. God sent prophecy of defeat and captivity, but the people continued to live as though God did not even exist.

Who Are the Main Players?

Amos and God's people

Digging In

Read 1:3, 6, 9, 11 and 13. What is the common phrase that God says about these sinful nations?

_____

Read 4:1. What does God call the women who hurt the needy and poor?

_____

In 5:4-6, who should the people seek?

_____

In 5:21, what does God hate?

_____

God sends destruction in chapter 7. What does He send in verse 1?

_____

What does He send in verse 4?_____ What is God going to do in verses 7-9? _____

Read what a plumb line is in the Glossary.

_____

In chapter 9, God sends destruction, then restoration. How will God restore the people and land? (verses 11-15)

_____

_____

Digging Deeper

Read the entire book of Amos. Then, on a separate sheet of paper, write a diary page as if you were growing up in those times. Tell what is happening around you. Be sure to add some hope for those who follow the Lord's commands.

Plant God's Word

Do two walk together unless they have agreed to do so?

— Amos 3:3

Surely the Sovereign Lord does nothing without revealing his plan to his servants the prophets.

— Amos 3:7

⭐

A Foreign Nation Destroyed

Where Are We?

The book of Obadiah

What Is the Big Picture?

The book is written by Obadiah. Edom is a nation of people from the line of Esau. Israel is from the line of Jacob. Edom treats Israel badly because of the events in Genesis between Jacob and Esau. Do you remember what happened?

Who Are the Main Players?

Obadiah and the people of Edom

Digging In

Read all of Obadiah. It has only one chapter.

Write three things that God will do to this nation of Edom.

_____

_____

_____

Write out verses 4 and 10.

_____

_____

_____

_____

_____

_____

⭐

Digging Deeper

Go back to Genesis and read about Jacob and Esau.

Read Numbers 20:14-22 and 21:4.

Plant God's Word

And the kingdom will be the Lord's.

— Obadiah 1:21

⭐

Don't Run from God

Where Are We?

The book of Jonah

What Is the Big Picture?

Jonah wrote this book. Jonah was chosen by God to
preach to a heathen city and call for repentance. Jonah was a
Jew, and Nineveh was a Gentile city. Jews and Gentiles hated
each other. Jonah did not want to preach to this city of people.
Jonah's life was saved when God provided the great fish;
otherwise he would have drowned. Then Jonah obeyed
God and Nineveh repented. Jonah became angry with
God for saving this heathen nation.

Who Are the Main Players?

Jonah, sailors on ship and the people of Nineveh

Digging In

Read Jonah 1-3. In 1:1-2, God called Jonah to go preach against
the great city of Nineveh. What did he say about Nineveh in
verse 2? _____

_____

In 1:3, Jonah _____ from the Lord. He went aboard a
ship and sailed for _____ to flee from _____ .

When a terrible storm came upon them, whom did the sailors
cry out to? (verses 4-5) _____

In verse 7, how did the sailors found out who was responsible
for the great storm that was about to break up the ship?

_____

★

After they threw Jonah into the sea, whom did the sailors cry out to instead of their own gods? (verse 14)

_____

How did God save Jonah from drowning in the raging sea? (verse 17) _____

Read Jonah's prayer again, in chapter 2:1-9. What do those who worship idols forfeit (give up)? (verse 8) _____

In 3:1-3, Jonah finally obeys God. In 3:5, 8, how did Nineveh react to Jonah's preaching? _____

Did God destroy the city because of its wickedness? (verses 10-11) _____

Digging Deeper

Read chapter 4. Jonah was angry because God saved the city of Nineveh. What did God ask Jonah in 4:4?

_____

In 4:5, why did Jonah sit outside the city of Nineveh? What did God provide for Jonah? (verse 6)

_____

In 4:7-9, why was Jonah angry then? _____

Read verse 10. Write God's answer to Jonah in your own words. _____

_____

_____

_____

Plant God's Word

I worship the Lord, the God of heaven, who made the sea and the land.
— Jonah 1:9

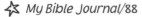

God Has a Plan

Where Are We?

The book of Micah

What Is the Big Picture?

Micah wrote this book. Micah lived at the same time as
Isaiah the prophet, and brought a similar message.
This book brings the message that God hates the sin but
loves the sinner. Christ's birth is foretold.

Who Are the Main Players?

Micah and God's people

Digging In

In 1:1-2, who is a witness against the people?

_____

In 1:5, why were Samaria and Jerusalem destroyed?

_____

Read Micah 5:2 and Matthew 2:1-6. Whose birth do these
foretell? _____

_____

Digging Deeper

Look up these verses to find these sins of God's people. Write
how you could commit these sins if you are not careful.

1:7 — Idolatry

_____

2:1 — Evil and wrongdoings

_____

2:2 — Covet [want] others' belongings and fraud to take these
     belongings dishonestly

_____

3:2-3,10 — Bloodshed (killing and wounding others)

_____

3:5-7 — Believing false prophets

_____

5:12 — Believing in witchcraft

_____

6:10-11 — Dishonest business practices *(see the part about the
     dishonest scales and weights)*

_____

6:12 — Violence, lying

_____

7:2 — Hatred among brothers

_____

7:3 — Bribery

_____

7:5-6 — No one is trustworthy, not even family members

_____

Plant God's Word

*He has showed you, O man, what is good. And what does the Lord
require of you? To act justly and to love mercy and to walk humbly
with your God.*

— Micah 6:8

Nineveh Punished

Where Are We?

The book of Nahum

What Is the Big Picture?

This book was written by Nahum. God sends a warning
to Nineveh. This happens over 100 years after Nineveh
repented and God saved it from His destruction. (Look back in
the book of Jonah to recall how God saved Nineveh.)
However, a few generations later, the people of Nineveh
are wicked and unbelieving again. This time they do not
repent, and God destroys the entire city.

Who Are the Main Players?

Nahum and the people of Nineveh

Digging In

Read all of Nahum.

In 1:2, God is a _____ and _____ God.

In 1:3, The Lord is slow to _____ and great
in _____. However, God will not leave the
_____ unpunished.

In 2:13, who is against Nineveh? _____

3:19 says Nineveh's enemies will _____ when it is
destroyed.

Digging Deeper

Look in Genesis 18 and 19 to find two other cities that were totally wiped out by God. _____

Plant God's Word

The Lord is good, a refuge in times of trouble. He cares for those who trust in him.

— Nahum 1:7

Questions for God

Where Are We?

The book of Habakkuk

What Is the Big Picture?

Habakkuk wrote this book. Habakkuk was troubled because sinners seemed to go a long time unpunished. He asked God why. God replied that it may seem a long time coming by human standards, but punishment is sure unless sinners repent. This book was written shortly before God's people were defeated and captured by Babylon. This is the punishment God is foretelling through His prophets.

Who Are the Main Players?

Habakkuk and God

Digging In

Read chapter 1:1-4. Habakkuk asks God, "Why don't You do something about all this sinning your people are doing?" Write out a situation in today's world where you might ask God the same question.

_____

Read 1:5-17. In verse 5, what does God say?

_____

Habakkuk's second question is in 1:12-17. He wants to know why one sinful nation is better than another. Why would God use a terrible nation like Babylon to punish His people?

_____

_____

Read Habakkuk's prayer in chapter 3. In verse 3, what covered the heavens in Habakkuk's vision?_____ What filled the earth?_____

Digging Deeper

Write out verse 2:14.

_____

_____

_____

_____

_____

Plant God's Word

The righteous will live by his faith.

— Habakkuk 2:4

God's Wrath

Where Are We?

The book of Zephaniah

What Is the Big Picture?

This book was written by Habakkuk. God will bring
His wrath down on sinful peoples, even though they are His
own chosen nation. God promises to restore His people.

Who Are the Main Players?

Zephaniah, God's people and other nations.

Digging In

In chapter 1, God's people are warned. In verse 14, what is
near? _____

In 2:7, God says He will take care of His own people. This
means that the Philistines do not have a chance of surviving
against God's people.

Read about Moab and Ammon in 2:8-11. These nations
insulted and threatened God's people.

Write out verse 11.

_____

_____

_____

_____

⭐

In 2:12, what will happen to the people of Cush?

_____

In chapter 3:1-7 God accuses His people of not obeying Him. Then, in 3:8-20, God promises to restore His nation. Read all of the verses.

Digging Deeper

Write out 3:20.

_____

_____

_____

_____

_____

Plant God's Word

Seek the Lord, all you humble of the land, you who do what he commands. Seek righteousness, seek humility; perhaps you will be sheltered on the day of the Lord's anger.

— Zephaniah 2:3

⭐

Rebuild God's Temple

Where Are We?

The book of Haggai

What Is the Big Picture?

Haggai wrote this book. God's people returned to Jerusalem after the Babylonian captivity. God wants His house rebuilt. The people are being selfish in taking care of their own needs first, but God tells them to change their thinking.

Who Are the Main Players?

Haggai, Zerubbabel and God's people

Digging In

Read all of this book.

In 1:8, how will God be honored? _____

In chapter 2, God promises to bring His glory into the temple.

In verse 9, how great will His glory be?_____ Also in verse 9, what will God grant inside His house? _____

In 2:19 what will God do from this day on?

_____

Read 2:20-22. What will God do to foreign kingdoms?

_____

In verse 23, what will God make Zerubbabel like?

_____

_____

⭐

Digging Deeper

Read some of these verses about signet rings:

Genesis 41:42

Numbers 31:50

Esther 3:10; 8:2,8, 10

Daniel 6:17

Plant God's Word

This is what I covenanted with you when you came out of Egypt.
And my Spirit remains among you. Do not fear.

— Haggai 2:5

The Future

Where Are We?

The book of Zechariah

What Is the Big Picture?

This book was written by Zechariah. Zechariah lived at the same time as Haggai. He brought a similar message as Haggai. Zechariah was a prophet and a priest. The book contains visions that God gave to Zechariah. God sent an angel to walk with Zechariah and give him God's Word.

Who Are the Main Players?

Zechariah, the angel, God's people and foreign nations

Digging In

Read 1:1-6. What does God say to tell the people in verse 3?

_____

Read about these visions that Zechariah saw:

1:7-17 — Man on a red horse. This was to tell of the condition of Israel in good times.

1:18-19 — Four horns. This was the four nations that scattered and persecuted God's people.

1:20-2 — Four craftsmen (carpenters). This told of God's judgments on those four nations.

Chapter 2 — Man with a measuring line. This tells about Israel restored to peace and prosperity.

Chapter 3 — Clean garments for a high priest. This means that God's people will be cleansed.

⭐

Chapter 4 — Gold lamp stand and two olive trees. This is Israel in the future, building God's temple.

5:1-4 — Flying scroll. This tells of a curse that goes out to sinners.

5:5-11 — Woman in a basket. This is a judgment against wickedness.

6:1-8 — Four chariots. Tells of God's judgments on foreign nations.

Who is walking and talking with Zechariah? (verse 1:12)

_____

Who is standing with God and Joshua in 3:1-4?

_____

In chapter 8, God promises to bless His people. Write out verse 3 here.

_____

_____

_____

Digging Deeper

Read in chapter 9 about God's judgment on Israel's enemies. Write out a sentence or two about what God will do in verses 14-17.

_____

_____

Plant God's Word

The Lord will be king over the whole earth. On that day there will be one Lord, and his name the only name.

— Zechariah 14:9

⭐

Hope Comes After God's Judgment

Where Are We?

The book of Malachi

What Is the Big Picture?

This book was written by Malachi. Malachi was the
last messenger of God until into the New Testament.
John the Baptist's ministry is foretold in Malachi.

Who Are the Main Players?

Malachi and God's people

Digging In

Read 1:1-5 about God's love for Israel. Who does God mention
from earlier Old Testament history?

_____

1:6-14 tells God's feelings about blemished sacrifices. God asks,
"Where is the _____ due me? If I am a master, where
is the _____ due me?"

2:1-9 tells that even God's _____ were not obeying and
honoring God.

In 2:16, what does God hate? _____

2:17-3:6 tells of God's coming judgment. In verse 2:17, what do
the people say that makes God angry? _____

_____

In chapter 3:7-12, the people are accused of _____
God. (verse 8)

In 3:13-18, those who listened and heard God's Word wrote out a _____ (verse 16) of remembrance. Whose names were on it? What does God say about these people who honored His name? (verses 17-18)

_____

_____

_____

Digging Deeper

Go to the book of Matthew and read 11:7-14. Now read Malachi 4:5-6. Can you figure out who John the Baptist is? Remember in 2 Kings 2:11-12 what happened to Elijah? Go back and read those verses.

Plant God's Word

"They will be mine," says the Lord Almighty.

— Malachi 3.17

New Testament

Matthew: A Gospel of Christ

Where Are We?

The book of Matthew

What Is the Big Picture?

Matthew wrote this book for the Jews who knew the
Old Testament very well and were looking for the Messiah
that God promised. Matthew, Mark, Luke and John are called
the gospels. These four books tell of the life of Christ.
Each writer tells the story a little differently.

Who Are the Main Players?

Jesus, Mary, Joseph and the 12 apostles

Digging In

Read chapter 1:18-24. An angel gives Joseph a message from
God. What is the message? _____

_____

Read chapter 2 about the Magi (wise men). What happens in
verse 13? _____

_____

Read chapter 4. Who tempted Jesus in 4:1-11? _____

_____

Write the words that Jesus used to fight off the tricks of the
devil in verses 4, 7 and 10. _____

_____

What did Jesus begin to do in verse 17? _____

_____

Chapters 8 and 9 tell of many of Jesus' miracles. Which is your favorite? _____

Chapters 26-28 tell about Jesus' arrest, trial, crucifixion, burial and resurrection. Read the three chapters. Write a poem to tell Jesus what these events mean to you.

Digging Deeper

Read chapter 1:1-17. Do you recognize some of these names from the Old Testament?

Chapter 13:1-14 tells why Jesus spoke in parables.

Read the parables in chapters 13, 18, 20-22. Draw a picture below of your favorite parable story.

Planting God's Word

Simon Peter answered, "You are the Christ, the Son of the living God."

— Matthew 16:16

Mark: A Gospel of Christ

Where Are We?
The book of Mark

What Is the Big Picture?
Mark wrote this book for the Romans. Jesus taught those around Him about the kingdom of heaven. He performed many miracles. Jesus showed how much He cares about people.

Digging In

John the Baptist prepares the way for Christ in 1:1-8. Read Isaiah 40:3 to compare with Mark 1:2-3. Then read verses 1-8 about John.

In 1:9-12, Jesus was baptized. Who baptized Jesus? _____ What came out of heaven when Jesus was baptized?
_____

In 1:12-13, where did Jesus go right after being baptized?
_____

In 3:13-19, Jesus appointed twelve apostles. Write their names here. _____
_____
_____

Why did Jesus call these men? (verses 14-15) _____

What miracle happened in 6:30-44?_____

What miracle happened in 6:45-52? _____

Read 8:27-30. What did Peter say about Jesus? _____

_____

Read about the transfiguration in 9:2-12. Who was there besides Jesus? _____

What does Jesus say will happen to Him in 10:32-34?

_____

Read 8:27-30 again. Then read 14:27-31 and 14:66-72.

Digging Deeper

Read some parables in chapter 4.
Read what happened to John the Baptist in chapter 6:14-29.

In 3:31-35, who are Jesus' mother and brothers?

_____

Who is greatest, according to 9:33-37? _____

What is the greatest commandment? (12:28-34)

_____

Planting God's Word

"Love the Lord your God with all…your mind and with all your strength." The second is this: "Love your neighbor as yourself." There is no commandment greater than these."

— Mark 12:30-31

Luke: A Gospel of Christ

Where Are We?

The book of Luke

What Is the Big Picture?

This book was written by Luke. Luke was a physician (doctor). The book tells a story of a perfect Christ, who cared about the people, taught about heaven, healed many and even cared about another dying man while He hung dying on the cross.

Who Are the Main Players?

Jesus, His followers, friends Mary and Martha and Peter

Digging In

Read 1:1-4 to see why Luke wrote this book. Notice that Luke says he has investigated very carefully.

Read 1:5-23 and 26-38. What did Mary and Elizabeth have in common? _____

Where did Mary go in 1:39? What happened in verses 41 and 42?

_____

Read chapter 2 about the birth of Jesus. Tell about the shepherds and angels rejoicing. Tell about Simeon and Anna.

_____

Tell about Jesus in the temple in verses 41-51. _____

What did Jesus often do during His ministry on earth? (5:16)

_____

Read 11:1-13 about prayer. Write out the Lord's Prayer in 11:2-4.

_____

_____

_____

_____

Digging Deeper

Read about miracles in the verses below. What are they?

4:31-37

_____

4:38-44

_____

5:1-11

_____

5:12-14

_____

Plant God's Word

Blessed rather are those who hear the word of God and obey it.
— Luke 11:28

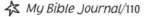
John: A Gospel of Christ

Where Are We?
The book of John

What Is the Big Picture?
This book was written by John. It gives information
to prove that Jesus is truly the Son of God. Jesus
has divine power, authority and knowledge.

Who Are the Main Players?
Jesus, the apostles and Lazarus

Digging In

Read 1:1-5. Where was Jesus in the beginning of time?

_____

Read 1:6-9. Who sent John and why?

_____

Read 1:19-28. Was John the Christ? _____

Who is the Lamb of God? (verse 29) _____

Read about Jesus' first miracle in chapter 2. Who asked Him to
do this miracle? _____

What did He say to her in verse 4?

_____

In chapter 3:1-21, Jesus teaches Nicodemus about the kingdom
of God. What does Nicodemus ask about being born again?
(verse 4)_____ Read Jesus' answer in verses 5-8.

In 4:1-26, Jesus teaches a Samaritan woman about forgiveness.
What does He say about water in verses 13-14?

_____

Read chapter 20 about some of the events that happened after
Jesus arose from the tomb. Write a short paragraph about
doubting Thomas (verses 20:24-29).

_____

_____

_____

Digging Deeper

Look up these verses to see when religious leaders opposed
Jesus many times:

7:25-41
7:45-52
8:42-47
8:48-59
9:13-41
10:22-39 (especially 33 & 39)
The plot to kill Jesus 11:45-57.
Whom did Jesus say this to: "Feed my sheep"? (21:15-19)

_____

_____

Plant God's Word

*Because you have seen me, you have believed; blessed are those who
have not seen and yet have believed.*

— John 20:29

*Jesus did many other things as well. If every one of them were written
down, I suppose that even the whole world would not have room for
the books that would be written.*

— John 21:25

⭐

The Beginning of the Church

Where Are We?

The book of Acts

What Is the Big Picture?

Jesus goes to heaven. Believers receive a gift.
The church begins. Saul is converted. Journeys
of those preaching about Christ.

Who Are the Main Players?

Peter, Paul, other believers and preachers of the gospel

Digging In

Read the account of Jesus' going into heaven (ascension) in 1:1-11. Imagine what it would have been like to have been there.

Read about the day of Pentecost in chapter 2. Write on the line below what Jesus' followers received, and what form it was in. (verses 2-4)_____Who preached a sermon on this day? _____

Read verses 2:42-47. To what were they all devoted?

_____

Read chapter 9 and learn about Saul's conversion and the beginning of his ministry.

Digging Deeper

Read the entire book of Acts, watching for interesting reports about these people:

Ananias and Sapphira – What did they do?

_____

Stephen – What happened to him?

_____

_____

Phillip and the Ethiopian – What did Phillip teach
this man about?

_____

_____

Dorcas – How did she serve God? What happened
when she died?

_____

_____

Peter's vision – What appeared on the sheet? (This is a story to
show that God wanted Peter to preach to Gentiles also, not just
to Jews. Salvation through Jesus is available to everyone, not
just a chosen few.)

_____

_____

Saul's conversion – What was his new name?

_____

_____

Paul's shipwreck – What bit him?

_____

_____

Plant God's Word

*Repent and be baptized, every one of you, in the name of Jesus Christ
for the forgiveness of your sins. And you will receive the gift of the
Holy Spirit.*

— Acts 2:38

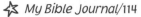

A Call to Be Righteous

Where Are We?

The book of Romans

What Is the Big Picture?

Paul wrote the book. But because of his bad eyes, he told
Tertius what to write (verse 16:22). This book contains calls
from God for His people to live right. This is similar to the
prophecy books of the Old Testament. God will bring His
judgment upon those who do not repent and live right for Him.

Who Are the Main Players?

Paul and God's people

Digging In

Read 1:1-7. Most of the New Testament letters begin with who
wrote the book, to whom it is written and sometimes why it
was written.

In 1:18-23, read about God's wrath against those who will not
live right. What is plain to man? (verse 19) _____

In chapter 3, we are told that righteousness comes from faith,
not by our own works. This is important to understand.
Nobody is perfect. Nobody can earn their way to heaven. But,
through faith in Christ Jesus (verse 22) all believers can be
righteous.

Chapter 5:1-11 tells how to have peace and joy. Through whom
can we have this? (verse 1) _____ Write out verse 1.

_____

_____

Read 5:12. Through whom did death enter the world?

_____

Read 5:21. Through whom do we have life? _____

In chapter 8, we are told that we have life through Christ and the Holy Spirit. Read 8:9 to find out whom we are controlled by now that we are followers of Christ.

In chapter 12, we are called to offer our bodies as _____(verse 1).

Read 12:9-21 about love. Write out verse 21. _____

_____

Digging Deeper

Read 8:28-39 to find out how we can be more than conquerors. Write out verses 38 & 39 of chapter 8.

Plant God's Word

And we know that in all things God works for the good of those who love him, who have been called according to his purpose.

— Romans 8:28

Matters of the Church

Where Are We?

The book of 1 Corinthians

What Is the Big Picture?

Paul wrote this book. Paul was a traveling preacher. He ministered to churches in many cities. Those churches didn't get to see Paul very often, but he wrote letters to them. Some of those letters make up the New Testament books. The letters were for encouragement or to straighten out some matters and problems in the churches. Paul also sent others to minister to the churches.

Who Are the Main Players?

Paul and the church at Corinth

Digging In

There were divisions in the church even in the early days. Read chapters 1-3 to find out how Paul wanted everyone to get along.

Read 6:7-8. What were the Christians doing to each other?

_____

In 6:9, Paul says that the _____ will not inherit the kingdom of God.

In chapter 10, Paul had to make many things clear, because the church was arguing amongst themselves. Read verses 14-22. The people are arguing about the Lord's Supper (communion). In verses 23-32, they argue about freedoms. Write out verse 32.

_____

In 11:17-22, why do the meetings of the church do more harm

than good?_____

In chapters 12-14, the people argued about who received
which Spiritual gifts?_____

What does Paul write in verse 12:12? _____

Digging Deeper

Read chapter 7 about marriage. Paul gave some rules and
some of his own opinions to the church about marriage.

Read chapter 8. What were the people in the church arguing
about? (verse 1)_____

In verse 1, it says knowledge puffs up, but _____ builds
up. Write out 8:3. _____

What lessons can we learn from 1 Corinthians concerning our
churches today? _____

Plant God's Word

Therefore, my dear brothers, stand firm. Let nothing move you.
Always give yourselves fully to the work of the Lord, because you
know that your labor in the Lord is not in vain.

— 1 Corinthians 15:58

⭐

A Minister for God

Where Are We?

The book of 2 Corinthians

What Is the Big Picture?

This book was written by Paul, to the church in Corinth again. Paul gives encouragement to the church. He also tells about himself and his ministry, his sufferings and health troubles. Through all that happens to him, Paul continues to preach the gospel and to love Jesus with all his heart.

Who Are the Main Players?

Paul and the church at Corinth

Digging In

Read 1:3-11 about God's care. In 1:10, whom can we set our hope in?

_____

_____

In 2:7, why must the sinner in a church be forgiven?

_____

_____

In 3:11, by what is the Old Testament covenant taken away?

_____

_____

In chapter 5:1 Paul tells of a heavenly dwelling. Write out verse 1.

_____

⭐

In chapter 5:11-21, we are told to help reconcile others to God. Read in the Glossary what "reconcile" means.

Digging Deeper

In 11:16 more of Paul's hardships (sufferings) are listed. In 11:28, what additional burden does Paul have?_____

Read chapter 12:1-10. When Paul pleaded for God to take away the "thorn in Paul's flesh" (a problem that bothered him constantly), what did God answer in verse 9? _____

Plant God's Word

Let him who boasts boast in the Lord.

— 2 Corinthians 10:17

Freedom in Christ

Where Are We?

The book of Galatians

What Is the Big Picture?

Paul wrote to clear up some misgivings in the church at Galatia. Paul wanted them to stop thinking foolishly and realize that they were now under "faith" and not the Old Testament law.

Who Are the Main Players?

Paul and the church at Galatia.

Digging In

Read 1:6-10. In verse 6, what were people turning to? _____Paul wanted to convince them that there is only one gospel, the gospel of Christ.

Read 3:26-29. Write out verse 26.

_____

_____

In chapter 5, Paul is trying to convince the church that they have freedom in Christ. What does he ask in verse 7? _____ _____In verse 9, what works through a whole batch?_____This means that a little confusion can get the people away from Christ.

Read 5:16-26 to see how to live a life by the Spirit.

Read chapter 6 to see what Paul said to the church in order to stay strong in Christ.

⭐

Digging Deeper

Read 1:11-23 about how Paul tells he was called by God.

Read 2:1-10 to see how Paul was accepted by the apostles. Remember that Paul used to persecute followers of Christ, and now he was preaching for Christ.

Plant God's Word

Let us not become weary in doing good, for at the proper time we will reap a harvest if we do not give up. Therefore, as we have opportunity, let us do good to all people, especially to those who belong to the family of believers.

— Galatians 6:9-10

In Christ

Where Are We?

The book of Ephesians

What Is the Big Picture?

This book was written by Paul. In this letter,
Paul is encouraging the church. There do not seem
to be problems in the church at Ephesus as in some
of the other churches to whom Paul writes.

Who Are the Main Players?

Paul and the church at Ephesus

Digging In

Read 1:1-14. Paul calls the church at Ephesus, "the _____
in Christ." Write out verse 3._____

_____

In verse 4, when were we chosen by God? _____

In chapter 2, we were once dead in our sins but are now
_____ in Christ. (verse 5)

Chapter 4 speaks of unity in the Body of Christ. Write out verse
16.

_____

_____

In 4:17–5:21, we are called "children of light." Write out 5:1 and
5:21._____

_____

_____

⭐

Digging Deeper

Read chapter 3, where Paul says he is preacher to the Gentiles.

Read 6:10-20.

Plant God's Word

Now to him who is able to do immeasurably more than all we ask or imagine, according to his power that is at work within us.

— Ephesians 3:20

Be Christ-like

Where Are We?

The book of Philippians

What Is the Big Picture?

Paul writes this letter while in prison. Even in chains,
he can serve God. He encourages the church at
Philippi to continue in their faith.

Who Are the Main Players?

Paul and the church at Philippi

Digging In

In 1:12-30, read about Paul's encouragement to the church to
rejoice in all situations and continue to have faith and serve
Christ.

In 2:1-11, Paul says in verse 5, "your attitude should be the
same as that of _____."

Read 2:12-18. Paul says to do everything without _____
or _____ (verse 14) so that you may become
_____ and _____ (verse 15), and in which
you _____ like stars (verse 15).

Read 3:12-4:1. Write out 3:14.

_____

_____

_____

_____

Write out 4:4.

_____

_____

_____

_____

Digging Deeper

In 4:2, which two women cannot agree with each other?

_____

What does Paul ask the church to do about these women?

_____

How can we avoid being like the two women in Philippians 4:2?

_____

Plant God's Word

Do not be anxious about anything.

— Philippians 4:6

☆

Rules for Holy Living

Where Are We?

The book of Colossians

What Is the Big Picture?

This book was written by Paul to the church at Colosse. Paul didn't preach there and had never visited (2:1). The church was probably one that came about when believers heard about another church in a nearby town. This church at Colosse was a strong church, filled with people serving God. Paul does not write to clear up problems, but to encourage the church.

Who Are the Main Players?

Paul and the Colossians

Digging In

Read Paul's thanksgiving and prayer in 1:3-14. Paul opens most of his letters with praises and prayers to God. Even when he is writing from prison, Paul praises God.

In 1:15-23, Paul writes of Christ's supremacy. Write in your own words who Christ is and where He came from.

_____

_____

In 2:6-23, from what regulations are we free? (verse 22)

_____

_____

⭐

Read chapter 3. Write out at least two rules for holy living that Paul gives in verses 1-17. _____

_____

_____

Write out at least two rules for Christian households in verses 18-25. _____

_____

Digging Deeper

Read chapter 4. Write out some of Paul's instructions to the church. (verses 2-6)

_____

In 4:10, where was Paul when he was writing this letter?

_____

In 4:7-9, who is Paul sending to encourage the church in person?_____

_____

In 4:16, with what church does Paul tell the Colossians to share this letter? _____

_____

Plant God's Word

And whatever you do, whether in word or deed, do it all in the name of the Lord Jesus, giving thanks to God the Father through him.
— Colossians 3:17

Devote yourselves to prayer, being watchful and thankful.
— Colossians 4:2

⭐

Please, God: Stand Firm

Where Are We?

The books of 1 & 2 Thessalonians

What Is the Big Picture?

Paul was persecuted and attacked for preaching the gospel in Thessalonica. He fled and ended up in Athens. Timothy met up with Paul in Athens. Paul sent Timothy back to the church at Thessalonica with a letter (1 Thessalonians) to encourage the church to stand strong. He later wrote a second letter (2 Thessalonians) to clear up misunderstandings about the first letter. Paul did his best to encourage all of the churches, even if he was not able to go there in person.

Who Are the Main Players?

Paul and the people of Thessalonica

Digging In

1 Thessalonians

In chapters 1-3, Paul tells of his ministry in the church at Thessalonica. In 2:2 Paul and the other preachers of the gospel meet with strong opposition in many places. They are persecuted, jailed and treated badly along the way. In 2:9, what do the preachers do in order to not be a burden to the churches?

_____

In 3:2, who did Paul send to the church in Thessalonica?

_____

In 3:6, of what did Timothy bring back good news?

_____

In 4:1, what is the church asked to do more and more?

_____

And, in 4:10, what is the church asked to do more and more?

_____

_____

Write out 4:11.

_____

_____

_____

2 Thessalonians

Read 2:13-17. What are we chosen through? (verse 13)

_____

Read 3:1-5. About what two things did Paul ask for prayer?
(verses 1 and 2)_____

Digging Deeper

Read all of 1 and 2 Thessalonians. Write out at least three ways
that Paul teaches us to live holy lives. _____

_____

_____

_____

Plant God's Word

*May he strengthen your hearts so that you will be blameless and holy
in the presence of our God and Father when our Lord Jesus comes
with all his holy ones.*

— 1 Thessalonians 3:13

Instructing the Church

Where Are We?

The books of 1 & 2 Timothy

What Is the Big Picture?

Paul wrote these letters to Timothy.
They are filled with instructions for the church, and
for Timothy as a minister of the gospel.

Who Are the Main Players?

Paul and Timothy

Digging In

1 Timothy

Read 1:1-2 to find out who wrote the book (letter) and to whom
the letter was written. _____

_____

1:3-11 tells about false teachers. What does Paul say about
these teachers in verse 7?

_____

Chapter 2 gives instructions on worship. In 2:1-2, for whom
should prayers be given?

_____

How are today's churches different from what Paul describes
in chapter 2?

_____

_____

<u>2 Timothy</u>

In 1:5, who gave Timothy his great faith?

_____

Write out 2:1.

_____

_____

Read 2:14-16, 22-24. How can be a workman approved by God?

_____

_____

Digging Deeper

Read 1 Timothy 1:1-20. What is the trustworthy saying Paul writes in verse 15?

_____

Read 1 Timothy chapter 4 about the instructions Paul gave to Timothy as a minister of the gospel, and chapter 5 about widows, elders and slaves.

Read chapter 6. In verses 3-10, what is the root of all evil?

_____

Read all of 1 and 2 Timothy to learn how to live a godly life.

Plant God's Word

For there is one God and one mediator between God and men, the man Christ Jesus, who gave himself as a ransom for all men — the testimony given in its proper time.

— 1 Timothy 2:5-6

Be a Teacher and Encourager

Where Are We?

The books of Titus and Philemon

What Is the Big Picture?

These books were written by Paul as letters to
Titus and Philemon. Paul instructs these ministers on leading
the churches and keeping the people holy.

Who Are the Main Players?

Paul, Titus, Philemon, Onesimus

Digging In

Titus

1:5-16 tells why Titus is on the island of Crete. He was to finish
the work in the church and appoint _____ in every town
(verse 5). List the qualifications of an elder.

_____

In chapter 3:1, to what are we to be subject?_____

Philemon

In verses 4-5, why does Paul thank God for Philemon?

_____

What can we learn from verses 4-7 about how we can conduct
ourselves today?_____

In verse 16, what was Onesimus before he left Philemon? How
is he better now?_____

As a _____ in the _____. (verse 16)

Digging Deeper

Read all of both books, since they are very short.

What did you learn by reading Titus?

_____

_____

What did you learn by reading Philemon?

_____

_____

Plant God's Word

They must be silenced, because they are ruining whole households by teaching things they ought not to teach — and that for the sake of dishonest gain

— Titus 1:11

Who Is This Jesus?

Where Are We?
The book of Hebrews

What Is the Big Picture?
This book was written to the Hebrews. It is not known who wrote it. The two themes of Hebrews are: "Who is this man called Jesus?" and "Living as a Christian."

Who Are the Main Players?
Jesus and the Hebrews

Digging In

Read chapter 1. Write out verse 3.

_____

_____

In chapter 2:1, why must we pay attention to what we are taught? _____

In verse 11, what are we called?

_____

Write out 2:18 about temptation.

_____

In chapter 3:2-3, who is Jesus greater than?

_____

In 2:7-11, what will we not enter if we do not believe? (verse 11)

_____

⭐

Read 4:14-5:10. What does God say in verse 5?

_____

In 8:1-2, where is our high priest?

_____

In 8:6, what is the new covenant?

_____

Read 9:11 about the greater and more perfect tabernacle. Is it made by man's hands? _____

In 10:5-7 and 15-18, who is our sacrifice? _____

Write out verse 18.

_____

_____

_____

Digging Deeper

Read 4:12. What is sharper than a double-edged sword?

_____

Which priest from the Old Testament is Jesus compared to in chapter 7?_____

Read chapter 11 about faith. Write what you believe faith is.

_____

Plant God's Word

Now faith is being sure of what we hope for and certain of what we do not see.

— Hebrews 11:1

Christian Living

Where Are We?

The books of James and Jude

What Is the Big Picture?

James was written by James. Jude wrote the book of Jude. Jude was a brother of James. (The book of Jude comes just before Revelation.) The book of James contains information and encouragement to living a Christian life. Jude gives a warning to the godless and encouragement for Christians.

Who Are the Main Players?

God's people

Digging In

<u>James</u>

Read James 1:1. Who wrote the letter? Who received it?

_____

Read 1:2-18. What should we consider joy? (verse 2)

_____

What develops perseverance? (verse 3) _____

In 1:13-15, does God tempt us?_____

In 1:19-21, man's anger does not bring about the _____ life that _____ desires.

In chapter 2, what is the favoritism that James says Christians shouldn't have? (verses 1-4) _____

What is an example of working for God, as in verses 15-16?

_____

Read chapter 3. What should we tame? (verses 7-8)

_____

Jude

Read all of Jude.

In verse 4, who has slipped in among the people?

_____

In verses 17-23, how can God's people stay pure in a sinful world? (verses 20-21) _____

_____

Digging Deeper

Read James 3:13-18. Which wisdom comes from heaven?

_____

Read James 4:13-17. In verse 17, who sins?

_____

Plant God's Word

Everyone should be quick to listen, slow to speak and slow to become angry.

— James 1:19

A Living Hope

Where Are We?

The books of 1 and 2 Peter

What Is the Big Picture?

Both books were written by Peter. They are letters to
Christians. We are encouraged to live with hope, live as God's
chosen people and to stay away from false teachers.

Who Are the Main Players?

God's people

Digging In

1 Peter

Read chapter 1. In verse 3, we have a new birth into
a _____ hope through the _____ of
_____.

In verse 7, what is worth more than gold? _____

In verse 13, how do we prepare for action? _____

Read verses 13-16 and write out verse 16._____

_____

In verse 22, how have we purified ourselves? _____

In chapter 2:1-3, what should we get rid of?_____

_____

Look up all of these words in a dictionary.

In 2:4-6, into what are we being built?_____

Read chapter 4. Write out verse 11.

_____

_____

_____

Write out verse 19.

_____

_____

2 Peter

Read 2:1-3 What harm do false teachers cause?

_____

Chapter 3 tells about the coming of the Lord in His time. Read verse 8 to find out how long a day is in God's time. What will happen in the day of the Lord? (verse 10)_____

Digging Deeper

Read 1 Peter 3. What is one rule that is given for husbands and wives? _____

In verse 8, we are to live in _____ with one another. Write the rest of that verse to show how we should be.

_____

In 1 Peter chapter 5, what is one rule given? _____

Read 2 Peter, chapter 1. Write out verses 5-7._____

Plant God's Word

Cast all your anxiety on him because he cares for you.

— 1 Peter 5:7

Outlining Books of the Bible

Where Are We?

The books of 1, 2 and 3 John

What Is the Big Picture?

These three books were written by John as if he were writing to family or friends. Read all three of these books and decide for yourself what the important things to remember are.

Digging In

A good way to find main points is to look at the subheads in your Bible. Most Bibles have these subheads. Example: In 1 John the subhead just before verses 1-4 is "The Word of Life." Read all 3 books of John and write one main point for each.

1. _____

_____

_____

2. _____

_____

_____

3. _____

_____

_____

☆

Read 1 John. Write at least three important points from the book._____

_____

_____

_____

_____

Read 2 John. What is John telling the receiver of this letter?

_____

_____

_____

This book is so short, there are no chapters or subheads.

Read 3 John. To whom is the book written and what is John trying to say?_____

_____

This, too, is a very short book.

Digging Deeper

Reread one of the books of John. Write a letter to your own church below. Tell the people the same things that John said in his letter.

Plant God's Word

And now, dear children, continue in him, so that when he appears we may be confident and unashamed before him at his coming.

—1 John 2:28

✫

A Vision of the Future

Where Are We?
The book of Revelation

What Is the Big Picture?
This book, written by John, is actually a big picture
of heaven and the judgment day of the Lord. It contains
mostly symbols, so it can be hard to understand.

Who Is the Main Player?
John

Digging In

Read chapter 1 to find these answers:

Who wrote the book? (verse 1)

_____

Who gave the vision for the book? (verse 1)

_____

What creature spoke to John? (verse 1)

_____

In verse 2, whose Word is said to be in this book?

_____

Read 1:7. Who will see Jesus coming on the cloud?

_____

Where did John see the visions and write this book? (verses
8-9)

In verse 17, what did John do when he saw Jesus?

In chapter 6, what did the Lamb open? How many of these were there? (verse 1)

In 20:7-10, who is thrown in a lake of sulfur? (verse 10)

Read chapter 21. What did John see in verse 1?

Digging Deeper

Write out 22:18-19.

Plant God's Word

Behold, I am coming soon! Blessed is he who keeps the words of the prophecy in this book.

— Revelation 22:7

In Conclusion

I completed *My Bible Journal* on:

_____

The most important thing I learned was:

_____

_____

_____

_____

My favorite Bible story is:

_____

My favorite book of the Bible is:

_____

_____

_____

My favorite Bible verse is:

_____

_____

Glossary

Abundance: there will be plenty of food and grain to go around. Joseph was to help store up 1/5 of all the food and grain during the seven years of abundance.

Adultery: unlawful relations between a married person and another person. God's nation is often called adulterous, because the people worship idols instead of God.

Altars: built platform on which to place offerings. Many kinds of offerings were burned on altars, while some were not burned.

Anoint: to pour or place oil on a person's head. The anointing was for priests, prophets and kings.

Anxiety: worries

Anxious: to be upset or worry

Apostle: one who is sent

Ark of the Covenant: This is the special place in which God's law is placed. There are many rules throughout the chapters of the Old Testament concerning the ark of the covenant. It is very special and very sacred.

Ascension: to ascend or rise. Jesus ascended into heaven.

Atonement: the bringing together again (restoring) of right relations between God and man after man has sinned. Ways of atonement were by sacrifices, offerings, prayers and repentance.

Beatitudes: often called the "be happy" verses

Birthright: a special privilege or "right" given to a firstborn son

Blameless: without blame, pure

Blemished: something that is not perfect. God commanded that perfect offerings (animals, etc.) be used for His offerings, not leftovers or blemished things.

✭

Blessing: an honor or special favor given. In the Bible, firstborn sons received a special blessing from their fathers.

Boast: to brag

Bondage: slavery

Census: to count people

Consecration: to be set apart. God set His people apart from the world. He had great plans for His people.

Consumed: totally destroyed. The prophets of Baal were totally destroyed by fire.

Covenant: a binding agreement; a promise

Covet: to very strongly want something that belongs to someone else

Curse: to swear at or try to bring evil on someone

Decree: a law or order given to the people

Deeds: the works we do for God

Descendants: the people of Abraham's family and God's race of people who will be born after Abraham

Discern: to make good judgements

Exile: to be taken away from home or country. God's people were captured and taken away from their country.

Famine: there would be no food. This famine was to last seven years. The grain and food that Joseph helped store up for the seven good years would feed the people for the seven bad years.

Fast: to go without food for a religious reason

Foreigners: people who live in a different country than your own. In this case, foreigners often tempted God's people to worship their false gods and to sin in many ways.

⭐

Forfeit: to give up

Forsake: to leave or abandon someone

Generation: all the children of a certain time. You are from one generation. Your parents are a different generation. The Israelite children grew to adulthood during the wandering in the wilderness, which meant a new generation of people entered the Promised Land.

Gentiles: those who are not born Jewish

Glean: to gather the grain left behind by reapers

Heathen: one who does not believe in God, or a whole nation that does not acknowledge the one true God

Humility: to not have too much pride

Idols: false gods

Idolatry: to worship false gods and idols

Iniquity: wrongdoing, injustice or sin

Integrity: an upright or moral person; one who does right

Kin: a relative, part of the family

Kinsman-redeemer: a man in the family who will marry a widow and give her children to keep her first husband's name alive. In Bible times, it was an honor to have children, so a widow without children was to marry another family member.

Lamentations: expressions of sorrow

Leprosy: a common disease in Bible times. In Naaman's case, his skin was covered with the disease.

Manna: the food God provided for His people. Providing this food was a miracle.

Mantle: a loose, sleeveless coat-type garment. This cloak is what Elijah put upon Elisha. It had a special meaning that told Elisha he was chosen by God.

⭐

Mediator: someone who comes between two or more parties or people to help find a solution to a problem

Miracle: an event (such as a healing) which cannot be explained by the known laws of nature

Mourn: to show great sorrow, as when a loved one dies

Nazirite: a person who is set apart for service to God. Read Judges 13:5 to find the rule about a Nazirite's hair.

Oppressed: to keep down by using unjust force or authority

Oracle: a statement or revelation given by God to a person

Ordination: the ceremony in which people are set apart for priesthood (Old Testament) and ministry (New Testament)

Parables: earthly stories with a heavenly meaning. Jesus used many parables in the New Testament.

Persecuted: when someone is cruel or mean to another

Persevere: to keep on trying, even in troubled times

Pestilence: the same as a plague

Pharisees: religious leaders in the New Testament. However, they failed to believe in the Christ that God promised to send.

Plague: a widespread affliction. This means that something bad happens to a lot of people, not just a few. In Exodus, the plagues happened to all of Egypt.

Plumb line: a string that has a weight on the end. The weight holds the string exactly straight. This line is used to make sure a wall is exactly straight. It is also used to find out how deep something is, such as a well.

Plunder: to steal. When armies defeated a nation, they stole things of value.

Potshard: a piece of broken pottery

⭐

Priests: those who teach God's will

Proclamation: a public announcement

Prosperity: to be successful or well off

Proverb: a short saying that tells a truth

Psalm: a religious song or poem

Purification: to become clean, stay clean, or get rid of sin and guilt

Quail: small, edible birds

Ransom: when money or something valuable is paid for release. We are ransomed from sin by Jesus' life.

Reapers: those who are picking or harvesting the fields, such as grain

Rebellion: to not accept the leadership of another, even to the point of violence

Rebuke: to reprimand, demand a corrective action, or criticize

Reconcile: to bring back. If we help others to reconcile to God, we are bringing them from sin to a life of loving and serving God.

Regulations: the same as rules

Resurrection: to be raised from the dead. All of Jesus' followers will be resurrected and will be taken to heaven.

Restitution: to give back what someone rightfully owns, or to pay for the lost things

Restrictions: limits. God set some special limits, or rules, about the Passover.

Righteousness: the same as "right-ness"

Sackcloth: a garment worn as a symbol of mourning or repentance

Salvation: the saving of people from evil and wrongdoing

⭐

Scribes: religious leaders in the New Testament. However, they failed to believe in the Christ that God promised to send.

Signet Ring: a ring that has a certain seal or design on it. A person in authority used the ring to stamp his seal on important papers.

Supremacy: the greatest

Tabernacle: a place of worship. God gave the Israelites every detail to make the tabernacle. It was moveable, so the people could take it with them as they traveled through the wilderness.

Temptation: to try to get someone to do what is wrong. The devil tempts us, just as he tempted Jesus in Matthew 4:1-10.

Tithe: one-tenth of a person's income that is to be set apart for a special use. God commanded one-tenth from His people.

Transfiguration: to be changed, glorified, illuminated (a glowing light around)

Ungodliness: not living for God — doing sinful things

Usurper: someone who takes authority without the right to do so. God did not raise up Abimelech up to be a judge.

Vengeance: punishment in return for a wrong

Vision: something seen with the mind, not the eyes. Certain people in the Bible received a message from God in visions, during a dream or trance.

Wrath: punishment and anger